Little Book
of Crap
No.2

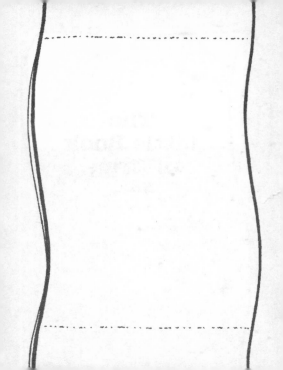

The Little Book of Crap
No. 2

Dr Neil Manson

BOXTREE

First published 2000 by Boxtree
an imprint of Macmillan Publishers Ltd
25 Eccleston Place London SW1W 9NF
Basingstoke and Oxford

www.macmillan.com

Associated companies throughout the world

ISBN 0 7522 7237 3

Copyright © Dr Neil Manson 2000

The right of Dr Neil Manson to be identified as the
author of this work has been asserted by him in
accordance with the Copyright, Designs and Patents
Act 1988.

1 3 5 7 9 8 6 4 2

A CIP catalogue record for this book is available
from the British Library.

Designed by Nigel Davies
Printed by Omnia Books Ltd, Glasgow

It has been hard, very hard. They said it couldn't be done. Well *they* would, wouldn't they? But finally, after many setbacks, *The Little Book of Crap No. 2* lies snug in your hand.

I've written this book just for *you*. Always have it about your person. Trust it and, on my life, *it will trust you*. When you feel sick, nervous, or dull, open it at random and the messages within are bound to be *exactly* what you need. Read a page. Read another. Close your eyes and feel safe and warm, like milk.

Read this book and make today the first day of the rest of your life.

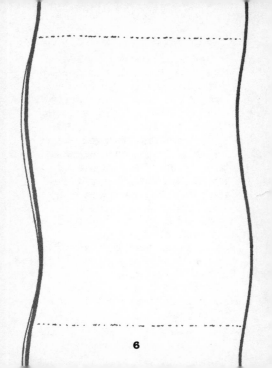

QUACK ADVICE
Worried about money?
Steal a duck,
chop off its head and bin it.
There, that's one bill
you've taken care of.

NOW THEN, NOW THEN
Worried about the future?
On your birthday get
someone to buy you
a large box.
Now you can live your life
in the present.

"BUT I READ THAT IT WAS OK TO TAKE THEM . . . !"

Osprey eggs make fine feng shui objects. Go to Scotland, steal some from a nest and then enjoy the peaceful uncluttered decor of one of Her Majesty's cells.

AH HA, JUST AS I THOUGHT

No one likes an unwelcome
surprise. Next time
you try something and fail,
do it again immediately.
You will almost certainly
fail again, but *you won't have
the unwelcome surprise.*
Now that *has* to be worth
something.

KICK OUT THE JAMS
Remember the old proverb,
"Jam tomorrow,
jam yesterday,
but never jam today."
If you have a teenage
guitarist in the house,
pin this on their
bedroom door.

SWISS BANK ACCOUNT HOSPITAL

If you want to be rich:
(a) become good friends
   with dynamic, rich
   successful people;
(b) pretend to have a fatal
illness and they will queue
up to load cash on you;
  (c) avoid spending the
   money on expensive
   medical treatment.
Remember, you may be *sick*,
   but you are not *ill*.

WHY ARE YOU ALL RABBITS?

Many children have
imaginary friends.
When they grow up, they
forget about them.
But this means that there
are literally *millions* of
imaginary friends who have
been left behind.
Think what your address
book will be like when you
tap this fantastic resource!
Happy talking.

INJURY TIME

Time is the great healer.
Strap a watch to a cut
or bruise and sit back
and wait! No need for
expensive medical bills!

THE ADVICE OF
FUR-KING HAL
Animal trappers whose
throats get irritated by
flying hair when they are
skinning their prey
find it very helpful to
repeatedly shout
"Fur Cough" at the top
of their voice.
Try it! See how it relieves
irritation.

AISLE BE BOUND
Go to a supermarket and
take what you want.
If challenged say, quite
forcefully, "What!
Don't you want people to
help themselves? Fine!
You fill the basket and
take it to my car then!
That's the last time I try
to show some initiative!"
Keep repeating this for as
long as is necessary.

I CAN SEE FOR METRES

The wise mountaineer
places his flag in the ground
when he gets a bit tired,
and calls that spot
"the summit".
He then goes home proud
of yet another success!
Be like that mountaineer.
Whatever happens you
have succeeded in
doing something!
Congratulations!

HAT-TRICK

Write down all the things
you want on pieces of paper.
Pop them in a hat.
Whenever you're feeling
down, pick one out.
Wonders!
You win every time.

WORDS FAIL ME

Do you ever feel
tongue-tied when trying
to express your feelings?
Then try using *words* like
everyone else, rather than
that ridiculous method
of making funny shapes
with your tongue.
Idiot!

YOU'RE THE ONE THAT I WANT

Why is the film
Grease so popular?
Though it may be dumb,
it has catchy songs.
No matter how stupid
you are, if you *sing*
what you say, it will
sound better!

IT'S NOT WHO YOU ARE
IT'S WHERE YOU ARE

If someone makes
a critical comment
about your weight,
remind them that weight
is relative and that
on the moon you would
weigh the same as
a basket of eggs.

ALWAYS LOOK ON THE BRIGHT SIDE

If you are feeling down,
look at the moon.
There!
You can't help looking on
the bright side, can you!

DARK SIDE OF THE MOON

If you are feeling down,
listen to Pink Floyd.
There!
You can't help
feeling down, can you!

PICTURE YOURSELF ON A BOAT ON A RIVER

Imagination is a powerful tool.

Next time you need to put up shelves but don't have a top-grade masonry drill, simply imagine the holes appearing. Now put up your shelves (but do remember to remove all breakable objects from the area).

KEEP AN OPEN MIND
Some people say
that oranges are not
the only fruit.
They're right!
Keep an open mind
as far as fruit is concerned.

A BRIEF HISTORY OF
THE LAST QUARTER

It is said that the
super-clever mathematician
Stephen Hawking has
an electric brain.

Wow!

Imagine what clever-clog's
leccy bill must be like!

WHO ME? AN INDUCTION

Think about it.
Every day you wake up,
have breakfast.
The more that happens
the more it is likely to
happen tomorrow.
So it is very likely that
you will live for ever.

YESTERDAY, ALL MY ROUBLES SEEMED SO FAR AWAY

There is a wise Russian proverb which says: "When it is dark it will always get darker, when it is light, it will get even darker still."

GO AHEAD,
ASK THE AUDIENCE
No need to appear on
stressful TV quiz shows.
You already have a million
hairs on your head, so you
are a million-hair!!
[Note, this figure may not be
remotely accurate.]

EGG 'EM ON
Encourage your friends
to do well.
Then spend the rest
of your life bitching
about them when
they succeed and
start hanging out with
the A-list.

MODERN RHYMES

If you cannot cope then
that's the time for hope —
or maybe dope. Nope?

HEALTHY BODY,
HEALTHY MIND

Take care of your body.
Keep it in a garage,
or under tarpaulin,
never out in the rain.

BE A FRIEND
OF THE EARTH

Don't worry about
the fact that we
devastate the environment.
Remember,
you are what you eat,
so if you eat greens,
you are green.

YES I REALLY AM THE ENVIRONMENT MINISTER

Greenhouse problem?
What greenhouse problem?
It can't be that important –
after all,
just how many of us
live in greenhouses?

WHAT'S IN A NAME

Do you want to get ahead?
Be in front?
Be top of the list?
Simple:
change your name to
Aaron Aardvark.

HAPPY BIRTHDAY

Every year you get a
year nearer your inevitable
death and an eternity of
non-existence.
But you didn't exist *before*
you were born and
each year you get *further*
away from that.
Yippee! Leave it behind,
for *good.*

ONE EYE WAS A LAD ...

Want to feel royal?
They say that in the
Kingdom of the Blind,
the one-eyed man is king.
So simply,
(a) gouge your eye out;
(b) find a Kingdom
of the Blind.
Oh, and remember that
sometimes the order of
things *matters*.

LOST THE THREAD
If a stitch in time
saves nine, think how many
a stitch *in advance*
would save!
What are you waiting for?
Get sewing!

LOADSAMONEY
Leave lots of toy money
around the house.
You will feel rich beyond
your wildest dreams.
Go on,
you can afford it!

STRAIGHT TO THE POINT

They say it is easier for a
camel to pass through the
eye of a needle than for a
rich man to enter the
Kingdom of Heaven.
If you're rich, don't worry.
With all your loot you can
pay for a very large needle
to be made and pushed
into the ground in some
Egyptian market-place.
Watch those camels fly
through the needle's eye!

HOW DO YOU SPELL P45?

Next time you are
caught taking a "sickie"
from work simply say
to the busybody,
"Absence makes the heart
grow fonder, you can't
criticize me for wanting
to be more fond of my
work, can you!"
Watch them seethe as they
realise you have won!

GUARD! GUARD!
Commuting to work
by train can make you
tense. Relax.
Rest your head on
your neighbour's lap.
Ask people for milk
and sweets. It is likely
that you will not have
to make this stressful
journey again (unless the
hospital has day-release).

IT ALL DEPENDS ON
HOW YOU LOOK AT IT

The unhappy person
sees obstacles,
the happy person
opportunities.
Why?
Oh, that'll be because
the first faces obstacles
where the second doesn't.

A PHOTO CAN'T LIE

If today seems a bit
dull, remember that in
the past everything was
in black and white.
You should think
yourself lucky!
That'll put the colour
back in your life.

NO I WON'T STOP
THIS WHISTLING

Have you ever heard
a sparrow moan about
not having enough money?
Have you ever heard
Mr Blackbird go on about all
his missed opportunities?
No, of course not!
We should learn from these
wise creatures, we should
whistle all day long.

I READ THE NEWS TODAY, OH BOY

Newspapers are full
of death and war.
Read seed catalogues
instead.

TOMORROW

Don't think about
the future.
Tomorrow rhymes
with sorrow,
today rhymes with hooray.

STICKS AND STONES
A sharp tongue
can hurt others.
Thankfully, virtually
everyone on this earth
has a kind of soft squidgy
damp one, so that's
one less thing to
worry about.

PHYSICIAN, HEAL THYSELF

Filling in a life insurance form? Cross out all those questions about illness and medical conditions and attach a note: "I think I am healthy therefore I am."
It works every time!

WORDS DON'T
COME EASY TO ME
Do you find it hard
to say "I love you"
to one you are fond of?
Go up to them and say,
"The Leith police dismisseth
us," a few times.
After that, if they are
still there, saying
"I love you" will be easy!

ALL THE
ROAD RAGE
Don't grow angry
when someone cuts you up
on the motorway,
grow sunflowers!

CAT IN HELL'S CHANCE

If you are bored,
why not test the old claim
that a cat has nine lives?
You will find your day
instantly lit up as you
invent super new ways of
doing away with Puss.

SURELY THAT
WON'T WORK?

If you compare yourself
to others you will almost
certainly be disappointed.
Let them compare
themselves to *you!*
Now who's top dog?

LOSE WEIGHT NOW,
ASK ME HOW

A happy man knows
his limitations.
A fat man eats
everything he can.
A happy fat man
either knows when to
stop or eats his limitations.
The question is,
which type are you?

MUMMY, I'VE FOUND A SOGGY CIGAR FLOATING IN THE WATER

We all like the British seaside but holidays are expensive. Problem solved: drink some water out the toilet, pour dirty sand into some sandwiches and enjoy a few days of "holiday tummy".

IT AIN'T NECESSARILY SO

Remember: everything
is possible. It's just
that some things aren't
possible *for you*.

REGRETS,
I HAVE A FEW

Made a mistake?
Don't worry, you have
the rest of your life to
dwell on it.

HEADS I WIN,
HEADS I LOSE

Don't worry if you face
some difficult decision.
If you decide correctly,
then your worry disappears.
If you decide wrongly, then
hey presto! Your worry
disappears as it turns
into deep regret.

NO TIME LIKE
THE PRESENT

You can't alter the future,
it hasn't happened yet.
You can't alter the past,
for it has gone.
You can't alter the present,
because altering things
takes time, and the present
doesn't last. So just what
are you going to do?

THOSE AREN'T MINE, AND I WAS AT CHURCH AT THE TIME, I THINK

Don't be ashamed of your dirty misdeeds. Just don't get caught, or, if you do, *lie, lie, lie* like your life depended on it!

TOP OF THE BOTTOM
OF THE CLASS

We all like to excel.
Next time you feel down
remember all the things
that you are very
very bad at doing.
Don't it feel good!

**DARE TO BE
DIFFERENT, GO ON!**
Few people ever admit
to being boring, even just
a little bit. So, if you
really want to stand out
from the crowd tell
everybody how dull you are,
preferably at length.

BE A BESTSELLER
If you want people
to like you, have the text
of a popular novel tattooed
on your skin.
Everybody likes reading.

IT IS ME
Happy is the man who
looks in a mirror and
see a happy man.
Put a picture of some
lucky bastard over your
mirror and see how
it makes you feel.
Yes. Just as I thought.

WHAT'S JAWS?
MINE'S A PINT

Cars are dangerous,
we all know it,
yet we all drive.
Alcohol is dangerous,
we all know it,
yet we all drink.
Nude alligator-wrestling
is dangerous, we all know it,
and yet we do not do it.
Why do we restrict
our lives? Go out,
get 'em off, get grappling!

DO I SATISFY YOU

If you are worried
about sex, remember
the song: "Birds do it.
Bees do it. Even educated
fleas do it." That's right,
they all can fly, and they
don't worry about sex.
So, best get your wings out.

HE MUST HAVE REALLY LIKED ME, I FEEL SO BAD

If you are feeling down, make a will. Even if you don't have much you can still gain a good deal of pleasure by leaving things to your enemies. Imagine how guilty they will feel. Once again, you are the winner (albeit a dead one).

DO NOT PASS GO

Who hasn't asked
the deep questions:
"Where am I going?
What is the meaning
of life?" Remember
the wisdom of the judge
(noted for his brevity):
"Prison. Twenty-five years."

ALL MY OWN WORK
If someone makes you
a nervous wreck,
make sure they give you
instructions on what to
do with it.

**IF YOU WANT
TO GET AHEAD**
Kidnap the headteacher
of your old school.

HEADS I LOSE
TAILS I LOSE

Are you faced with
a difficult life-choice?
Toss a coin. Not once,
it would be stupid to
base life-choices on the
toss of a coin. No.
Toss a coin *instead*
of whatever it was
you were going to do.
Life will pass, eventually.

I WILL NOT TRY
TO BE A BETTER PERSON

Every New Year
we all make resolutions
but don't keep them.
Next year, why not resolve
to do the opposite of
what you intend,
then you'll probably succeed.
Hurrah!

SWINGS AND
ROUNDABOUTS

The worse your life becomes,
the easier it is to imagine
ways in which it could
be better. There!
At least that's got easier.

IT'S GOT A VERY MOROCCAN FEEL TO IT

We can feel very anxious about the standard of our home decor. Worry no more. Smash up the furniture, smear brown paint over the walls and windows, and wait for *dirty-cell protest* chic to come into vogue.

IF AT FIRST
YOU DON'T SUCCEED . . .

If you fail to get a job,
don't worry, your failure
is somebody else's success.
Pretend you are that person.

. . . TRY, TRY AGAIN
Better still,
change your name
to theirs and turn up
early on Monday.
They will have some
explaining to do when they
arrive on time and
they are already at work.
They may even get sent
away. You WIN! You WIN!!

**BUT THIS IS THE
21ST CENTURY, ISN'T IT,
OFFICER?**
If your computer crashes,
take heed and learn
a lesson: don't ever let
your computer drive
your car again.

HERE'S A TIP FOR YOU

All things come to those
who wait. This is why
waiters and waitresses
have the most things.

WORDS OF SENSE

We all have a sixth sense –
nonsense.

LIFE'S WHAT YOU MAKE IT

Life is exactly the same
for all of us. The super-rich,
well-liked, healthy person
has to get through the same
miserable hours as the rest
of us. They have the same
number of legs and arms.
They may enjoy life more,
but so what! What's
enjoyment anyway?
Who needs it? Not you,
obviously, you seem to get
by quite well without it.

**THIS IS YOUR
CAPTAIN SPEAKING . . .**
Don't worry about crashing
when on a plane flight.
Just think, you will
experience things which
most people never will.
What an *opportunity*!

SPACE,
THE FINAL FRONTIER

We all want more space,
in our homes,
in our gardens.
But space is limitless. Look
up in the night sky and
point – claim whole star
systems as your own.
Now you really have some
room for storing all the
rubbish you've amassed
over the years.

NOW YOU SEE IT, NOW YOU DON'T

Every person is unique,
just like every tiny
snowflake.
Next time it snows,
catch a snowflake in your
hand, watch it melt.
That is how important you
and your life are.

TREES ARE GOOD,
TREES ARE GOOD

Make friends with a tree,
a tree is for life, not just for
Xmas. Except Xmas trees,
of course.

YOU GET THE SACK,
I'LL GET THE BRICKS

Remember: a dog is for life,
not just for Xmas. Except
Xmas dogs: they're just
presents to be thrown away
– after Xmas, *obviously*.

I'M SORRY,
COULD YOU SAY THAT
AGAIN

It is hard to say that
you're sorry.
True enough.
So *don't do anything wrong*,
and you won't need to.

GET IN THE VAN, PLEASE, SIR

People can't help
reacting well to a laughing,
smiling face.
Next time you are stopped
by a traffic policeman,
smile broadly, then laugh
and laugh till you can
laugh no more.

I *SAW* HIM,
NO I REALLY DID

As children we all believed in Father Christmas. There is no reason why you cannot *start* to believe in him again. Simply ask your mum and dad to start systematically lying to you round about Xmas time.

HEALTHY BALANCE: IT'S A WAY OF LIFE, NOT A BREAKFAST CEREAL

They say that it is hard
to balance all the different
demands of life:
job, family, friends,
selfish interests.
But it is *not* hard to
balance these if you *have*
no job, family or friends.
Be completely selfish and
your life will be in harmony.

ZENOPHOBIA

A Zen student once
inquired of the Master:
"A cat has holes in its fur
just where its eyes are:
is that not a miracle?"
The master replied,
"You've not actually thought
this through, have you?"
The student then admitted
that he had not.
Ask yourself: Are you the
student? The master?
The cat?

GIANT STEPS
ARE WHAT YOU TAKE
You can step outside
your house. You can,
if you want, step outside
a moving train.
But you can't step
outside your life.
Best get on with it, then!
(Incidentally, the moving
train thing isn't to be
recommended.)

WALKING
ON THE MOON

On the moon you can
leap as high as a house.
Experience the joys of space
travel by jumping over a
doll's house whilst eating
anchovy paste from a tube
and weeing in a bag.

CHANGING ROOMS
WITHOUT THE BUDGET

If you are in a negative
frame of mind, alter
your environment.
Use flowers and
aromatherapy. If you
can't afford this, just
close your eyes and
pretend the changes
have been made! This is
just as good, if not better!

TUNE IN, TURN ON, DROP THE REMOTE DOWN THE SETTEE

Watch telly. A lot.
Studies have shown that
while they are watching
telly, people forget
their problems.
Hopefully, when *EastEnders*
is over, all your troubles
will be over too.

WATER, WATER, EVERYWHERE

The albatross was
a good omen for mariners.
Yet we never see them
flying over our modern
cities. Is this a *sign*?
Are we *doomed*?

EASY PEASY
LEMON SQUEEZY

Why do we spend our lives
wanting things?
If you stop wanting,
you will never *fail*
to get *what you want.*

C U LATER
Saying goodbye to
a loved one can be hard.
No problem.
Say "cheerio" instead.

I DIDN'T BOTHER
TO WRAP IT

What do you give the man
who has everything?
Nothing. That is definitely
something that he doesn't
have already.

ALL I WANTED
WAS TO GIVE PEACE
A CHANCE

Being tranquil is hard work.
It needs discipline,
organisation and a strict
routine. You have to *work*
at it and you will probably
not have the stamina.
Start worrying now.
Have you got what it takes?

NO MORE F-WORDS

The word "failure"
is not in my dictionary.
Nor need it be in yours,
with judicious use
of scissors.

SO NICE TO MEET YOU, ISN'T IT

The happy person
litters their speech with
those little extra phrases
that make life so jolly:
"My, how nice!",
"How super", "You're not
still earning *that*, are you?",
"I didn't know they still
made those trainers."

"IS THERE ANOTHER BOOKMAKER'S NEARBY?"

It's easy to win money. Simply bet that Xmas will fall on 25th December and then you will win whether it snows or not.

WHERE'S THE
MEDICAL DICTIONARY?
Do you constantly think that
you suffer from some
ailment or other?
Don't worry! You do!
It is called hypochondria.

ALL THAT PEACH MUSH
HAS RUINED MY RACKET

People like fruit. People like
sport. But very few sports
use fruit. There is an
opportunity here for
someone, someone like you!

REMIND ME, JUST WHAT WAS THE LIFE EXPECTANCY IN THE ANCIENT WORLD?

People who are not ill will not say that they are ill. So if you never say that you are ill you will never be ill. That is the secret of health, long understood by the ancients.

SLEEP ON
SHEETS OF PAPER

If you have trouble fitting
everything into your waking
hours simply carry them
over into sleep and *dream*
that you have done them.
There is nothing like waking
up to an empty "in" tray!

THE SONG OF
THE MOCKINGBIRD

Ancient Oriental wisdom
tell us that our lives are
governed by an inner spirit
force called *mi-kei*.
If you want to be loved you
must avoid taking the *mi-kei*
out of others.

DON'T SIT NEXT TO
THE LOTUS EATERS

Statistically, it is extremely
unlikely that you are the
best at anything, or even in
the top ten per cent.
Success, like bad breath,
is something other
people have.

**THAT CAR LOOKS LIKE
A TINY MODEL...
... WOW, IT'S A FORD
MOND...**
If, unluckily, you find
yourself plummeting from
an aeroplane just keep
saying "I can *fly*, I can *fly*."
The drop will pass in
no time at all.

GRAMMAR
KNOWS BEST

It is comforting to know
that all those worrying
"what if this happens",
"what if that doesn't",
will soon be changed into
"if only this hadn't", and
"if only that had".

IT'S NOT ME SAYING THIS, IT'S THE RADIO IN MY HEAD

If you feel overcome by anxiety whilst waiting for an important interview, say quietly to the other candidates, "I collect knives," grin wildly and keep saying, "You killed the Princess and now I know where you live." That should put them off a bit.

BACK TO NATURE

Organic food is only the beginning. To *really* get in tune with nature you need eat soil and wait for the sun's rays to make you grow big and strong.

LEAVE ALL AEROSOLS, EXPLOSIVES AND ANXIETY BEHIND

If you are feeling very anxious, picture a peaceful seaside scene. The sea is calm and the waves lap on the shore. But wait! Clouds on the horizon! And where are all the birds? The sea looks dark and foreboding. Everyone has gone now, you are *alone, alone, alone* with the howling wind . . . Don't let your anxious mind go a-wandering. *Deal* with it.

HAVE YOU DROPPED OFF?

A calm, serene daydreaming person makes a useless sexual partner. Their mind will be on wind-chimes, kittens and streams, so you might as well just not bother.

COUNT YOUR BLESSINGS

If you feel unloved,
regularly sniff ground
pepper up your nose.
People will be constantly
blessing you.

**ANY MORE ROOM IN
THERE, MR OSTRICH?**
If it looks like your
chances of success are slim,
don't worry.
Statistics can easily
be *ignored*.

I THOUGHT SO

Remember, the happy man
never thinks he will be
other than he thought he
would have been had he
not thought he would have
come to be the way he
thought he was.

ONE STEP AT A TIME

We all think too much.
Let your feet guide you
where *they* want to go.
Spend long happy hours
window shopping for shoes.

BIG HUGS

Remember to respect other people's boundaries. They are never as big as people like to think they are – so go on, give them a squeeze.

BIG JUGS

Old Lancashire folk wisdom has it that a simple water jug will bring luck to your home. Whenever you want to pour some liquid, find it and say: "Lucky I had this jug."

I CAN'T GET ME NO SATIS-FAC-TION

You can't always succeed
in getting what you want.
But you can always succeed
in wanting what you
haven't got!

IT'S OK, I'M A LEO

Beautiful creatures can do you no harm. Creep into the lions' enclosure at the zoo, and marvel at their natural majesty. Share your feelings with them and they will share theirs with you!

THAT'S YOUR HEAD,
THOSE ARE CLOUDS,
YOUR MOVE

A sage once said, "It is
better to spend your life
imagining yourself to have
succeeded in all sorts of
fantastical things than to get
on with the ordinary hassle
we all have to put up with."

TUNES HELP YOU
Breathing is at the
heart of life.
The happy man always
remembers to breathe.

**GOLLY, IT'S *BETTER*
THAN MORPHINE**
You can't get hurt
if you are dead.

FUTON WALL-HANGINGS ARE ALL THE RAGE

If your employer tries to make you work overtime, simply reply, "I can't do that, the aliens living in my brain will not allow it. They insist that I go home to feed them the chalky fluid which nourishes them." They will not ask again, believe me. Not once. Not *ever*.

THE NIGHTS ARE DRAWING IN

Winter nights
can seem long.
That is because they *are*
long. Go to sleep like
everyone else and stop
bleating on.

LORD OF THE FLY

They say that know-alls
are full of hot air!
How true.
Have fun watching
the know-all rising up
in the air like a balloon.
Pelt him with sharpened
stones till he comes down
to earth deflated!

DRESS TO IMPRESS

Worried about keeping up with the latest fashions? Cut out pictures from the latest fashion magazines, paste them into a scrapbook with the words "My Clothes" on it. Wear your usual has-been drab attire, but carry the book around and show people at every available opportunity.

CLEANING TIME
Your future lies
open before you, your past
left behind you like
a snail trail. Have you
never thought of clearing
that mess up!

I WILL NEVER
EVER EAT CHOCOLATE
AGAIN

When you are angry
with someone make a large
chocolate model of them and
stuff it all in your mouth.
Hold it there till it melts and
then gradually dribble them
it into the gutter.
Do you *still* feel angry?
Not any more, I'll bet!

MAN'S BEST FRIEND

Many a person has
found that a dog gives
them love and affection.
But not postmen. The lesson:
if you are lonely,
don't buy a postman,
get a labrador.

RUM AND COKE
ON THE ROCKS

You are the captain
of your ship as you
voyage through life.
It's a shame that the ship
is rickety, rudderless
and that the sea is full
of rocks. Ah well,
there's always the rum.

THIS COULD BE THE LAST TIME

Imagine that today is the last day of your life. Savour the rich joy. Every blade of grass looks important, doesn't it? Or not. Alternatively, savour the desperate feelings of worry about not having really achieved very much. Think about all those things you'd like to have done but now never will.

IT'S HERE, IN PRINT
Each day pretend
that something trivial
but good happened to you.
"I found 10p." "I saw a
chaffinch coughing up a
worm in an amusing way."
Make a note of it.
Ten years later you will not
remember whether these
things happened or not,
and you can just assume
that they all *did* happen.
Happy memories!

HOW DID THIS GET IN HERE?

I can't recall who said:
"Don't trust self-help books.
Their authors are not
interested in you.
They will peddle useless
trivia and use your
gullibility and worries to line
their own smug pockets."
Wise words indeed, they
may even be my own.

THAT CAT'S GOT NO TAIL

A wise man
once said that no man
is an island:
what about
the Isle of Man?